Kids' CHRISTMAS cookbook

Brittany and Erica Sindeldecker

BARBOUR
PUBLISHING

ISBN 1-59310-887-7

Cover image © Getty Images/Food Pix

Published by Barbour Publishing, Inc., P.O. Box 719, Uhrichsville, Ohio 44683, www.barbourbooks.com

Our mission is to publish and distribute inspirational products offering exceptional value and biblical encouragement to the masses.

Member of the
Evangelical Christian
Publishers Association

Printed in Canada.
5 4 3 2 1

CONTENTS

Morning Munchies 7

Meals and More 23

Thirst Quenchers 61

Oven Delights 79

No-Bake Treats 109

The recipes in this cookbook are yummy, creative, and fun. Most of them are very quick and easy to make; but some require chopping, cooking, and baking, so you should ask an adult to help you with them. Have lots of fun with your family and friends as you create and eat these special holiday treats designed just for you!

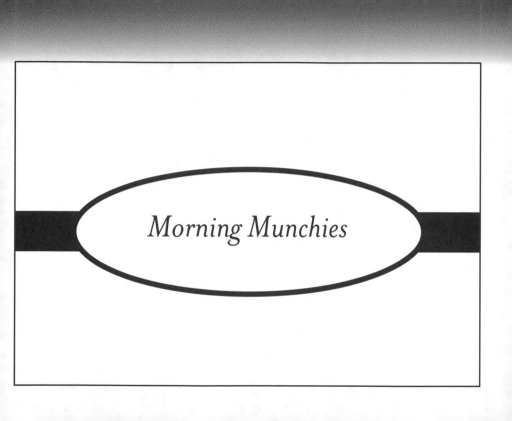

Legend of the Snowflake

D. M. BARIBAULT

A creation from heaven,
Each one is unique.
A long way to fall,
No sound it will make.
A shining, glistening snowflake.

Biscuit Coffee Cake
(from Debbie Sindeldecker)

2 cans buttermilk refrigerator biscuits
⅓ cup brown sugar, firmly packed
¼ cup butter, melted

1 teaspoon cinnamon
⅓ cup pecans

Preheat oven to 350 degrees. In a lightly greased 9x9-inch pan, arrange biscuits, overlapping edges. Combine remaining ingredients and spread evenly over biscuits. Bake for 15 minutes or until done.

Cheesy Sausage Balls

3 cups baking mix
1 pound ground sausage
½ cup milk

1 tablespoon parmesan cheese, grated
4 cups cheddar cheese, shredded
1 teaspoon parsley flakes

Preheat oven to 350 degrees. Mix all ingredients together in a bowl. Form into 1-inch balls and bake on a greased cookie sheet for 20 minutes or until done. Makes about 90 balls.

Cinnamon Biscuits

4 cans refrigerator biscuits   ¾ cup butter
1½ cups sugar   2½ teaspoons cinnamon

Preheat oven to 350 degrees. Cut each biscuit into quarters. Combine ½ cup
sugar and 1 teaspoon cinnamon in a bowl. Roll biscuits in cinnamon and sugar
mixture, making sure they are evenly coated. Grease a bundt cake pan and drop
biscuit pieces in the pan, keeping them evenly distributed. Mix 1 cup sugar,
butter, and 1½ teaspoons cinnamon in a small saucepan. Bring to a boil. Pour
over biscuits and bake for 45 minutes or until done. Let cool and flip over on a
plate. Pull apart to eat.

Cookie Cutter Toast

1 slice of bread
Butter

Peanut butter (optional)
Jelly

Toast a piece of bread. Using a Christmas cookie cutter, cut toast into desired shape. Spread with butter or peanut butter and favorite jelly.

Cutout Doughnuts

1 cup sugar
3 eggs, beaten
4 cups flour
¼ teaspoon cream of tartar
2 teaspoons baking powder

1 cup milk
1 teaspoon vanilla
Pinch of nutmeg
Powdered sugar

Beat together sugar and eggs until foamy. In a separate bowl, mix flour, cream of tartar, and baking powder. Add ½ flour mixture and ½ cup milk to eggs. Stir well. Pour in remaining flour and milk. Stir well. Add vanilla and nutmeg. Stir well, but do not make dough too stiff. Roll dough out on floured surface with a rolling pin until about ½ inch thick. Cut with a cookie cutter, then fry in hot oil until lightly browned. Sprinkle with powdered sugar.

Fluffy Eggs

8 eggs

¼ cup milk

Salt and pepper, to taste

In a bowl, beat eggs until no white shows. Add milk, salt, and pepper to eggs, and mix together. Pour into a frying pan, cooking over medium heat. Stir eggs until fluffy and creamy, making sure they do not stick to the pan. Place on a serving dish. Good with orange juice.

Four-Layer Breakfast Dish

1 pound ground sausage
4 eggs
¼ cup milk

1 can crescent rolls
2 to 3 cups mozzarella cheese,
    shredded

Preheat oven to 350 degrees. In a frying pan, brown sausage; drain excess fat.
Beat eggs and milk together. Put rolls in the bottom of a 9x13-inch buttered
casserole dish; layer sausage and egg mixture, and top with cheese. Bake for 30 to
50 minutes, until eggs are not runny.

Fruit Pizza

1 package refrigerated sugar cookie
    dough
1 (8 ounce) package cream cheese
12 ounces whipped topping
½ cup sugar

½ teaspoon vanilla
Mandarin oranges
Fresh fruit: strawberries, kiwi,
    pineapple, blueberries, banana

Preheat oven according to directions on cookie dough package. Cut cookies in ½-inch slices and arrange on a pizza pan, pressing together to make crust. Bake for 15 to 20 minutes or until done. Combine cream cheese, whipped topping, sugar, and vanilla in a bowl. Stir until smooth and spread over cooled cookie crust. Arrange fruit in layers on cookie crust. Cut into slices.

Fruity Bagel

1 bagel, any kind
2 tablespoons cream cheese, any
  flavor

Fruit slices (any fruit)
Powdered sugar

Cut a bagel in half and spread cream cheese on each side of the bagel. Place fruit on top and sprinkle with powdered sugar.

Muffins

3 eggs
1 cup milk

1 cup flour
½ teaspoon salt

Mix all ingredients in a bowl. In a greased muffin pan, fill each cup ½ full. Place muffins in a cold oven. Heat to 450 degrees and bake for 30 minutes. Serve with jelly, jam, or preserves. Makes 12 muffins.

Skillet Ham and Potatoes

2 tablespoons butter
1½ cups frozen shredded hash browns

½ pound ham, diced
Shredded cheese

Melt butter in a skillet. Add hash browns and cook over medium heat for about 10 minutes, making sure not to let them stick to the bottom. Leave hash browns in the skillet and add ham. Top with cheese. Reduce heat to low and cover the skillet until cheese melts.

Sweet Toast

12 large eggs
½ teaspoon cinnamon
2 tablespoons milk
1 loaf white bread, sliced
Vegetable oil

Butter (optional)
Maple syrup (optional)
Peanut butter (optional)
Powdered sugar (optional)

Beat eggs lightly. Add cinnamon and milk. Whisk with a fork. Dip bread in egg mixture, evenly coating both sides. Place in a heated skillet coated with vegetable oil and fry until both sides have browned. Top with butter, maple syrup, peanut butter, or powdered sugar.

French Toast—PB&J Style

12 slices bread
Peanut butter
Jelly, flavor of your choice
3 eggs

¾ cup milk
2 tablespoons butter or
    margarine

Spread peanut butter on six slices of bread; spread jelly on other six slices of bread. Put together to form sandwiches. In a bowl, lightly beat eggs; add milk and stir. Melt butter over medium heat in a large skillet. Dip sandwiches in egg mixture, then place in the skillet and brown on both sides.

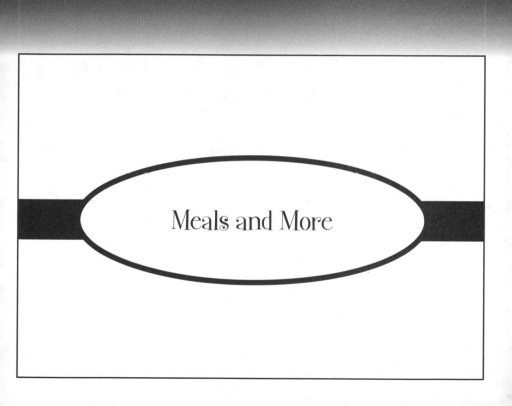

Meals and More

The Candy Cane

AUTHOR UNKNOWN

What do you see?
Stripes that are red
Like the blood shed for me.

White is for my Savior
Who's sinless and pure!
"J" is for Jesus My Lord,
That's for sure!

Turn it around
And a staff you will see.
Jesus my shepherd
Was born for me!

Apple-Cranberry Sauce

4 apples
1 cup cranberries

1 cup water
4 tablespoons honey

Wash, core, and chop apples. Boil apples and cranberries in water in a 1-quart saucepan until apples are tender. Add honey and stir. Serve warm.

Applesauce

4 apples
1 cup water

3 tablespoons honey
Ground cinnamon

Wash, core, and chop apples. Cook apples and water in a medium saucepan over medium heat until apples are tender. Add honey and stir. Pour into a serving dish and sprinkle with cinnamon.

Bacon Dip

16 ounces sour cream
½ teaspoon onion powder
1 (16 ounce) package ready-to-serve
   bacon

½ cup cheddar cheese, shredded
1 cup lettuce, shredded
1 cup tomatoes, chopped

Mix sour cream and onion powder together and spread in a 9-inch pie plate. Heat bacon as directed on package and cut into small pieces. Sprinkle over sour cream mixture. Top with cheese, lettuce, and tomatoes. Serve with crackers.

Bacon Sausage Bites

1 package ready-to-serve bacon   1 package mini sausages

Preheat oven to 400 degrees. Cut bacon in half and wrap around sausages. Use a toothpick to hold bacon in place. Place on a greased baking sheet and bake for 15 minutes.

Baked Corn
(from Cheryl Royer)

¼ cup butter, melted
1 box cornbread mix
1 can creamed corn

1 can whole kernel corn, drained
2 eggs, beaten
3 tablespoons milk

Preheat oven to 400 degrees. In a mixing bowl, blend butter with cornbread mix. Add corns, eggs, and milk; stir until well blended. Pour into a greased 2-quart baking dish and bake for 30 minutes.

Broccoli Bake

1 (10 ounce) package frozen chopped
broccoli, thawed
⅓ cup cheese, cubed

14 butter crackers, crushed
1 tablespoon butter

Preheat oven to 350 degrees. In a mixing bowl, stir broccoli, cheese, and half of the crackers until well blended. Pour into a 9x9-inch casserole dish. In a small bowl, stir the remaining crackers and butter; sprinkle over the broccoli mixture. Bake for 45 minutes.

Celery Sleighs

1 stalk celery
Peanut butter
Cinnamon candies

Raisins (optional)
Mixed nuts (optional)

Wash celery and cut off ends. Cut celery into 4- to 6-inch lengths. Spread peanut butter on inside of celery. Top with candies, raisins, or nuts.

Chicken Casserole

1½ cups chicken (or turkey), cooked and diced

1½ cups elbow macaroni, uncooked

1 cup cheddar cheese, shredded

1 (10½ ounce) can cream of chicken soup

1 cup milk

½ teaspoon salt

Preheat oven to 350 degrees. Mix all ingredients together in a bowl. Pour mixture into an ungreased 2-quart casserole dish. Cover with foil and bake for 1 hour. Serves 4 to 6.

Chicken 'n Noodles

1 (5½ ounce) package of butter noodles
1 (10½ ounce) can condensed cream of
   mushroom soup

2 cups chicken (or turkey), cooked
   and diced
1 (10 ounce) package frozen
   chopped broccoli, thawed and
   drained

Preheat oven to 350 degrees. Prepare noodles as directed on package. Drain.
Stir in cream of mushroom soup, chicken, and broccoli. Pour into an ungreased
2-quart casserole dish. Cover and bake for 25 to 30 minutes or until broccoli is
tender. Makes 4 to 6 servings.

Chili

1 pound ground beef
1 small onion, chopped
1 (16 ounce) can kidney beans
1 (14½ ounce) can stewed tomatoes

½ teaspoon salt
½ teaspoon pepper
1½ tablespoons chili powder

Brown ground beef and onion in a large skillet. Drain fat. Add remaining ingredients and cook on medium heat for 45 minutes, stirring often.

Cinnamon Pears

1 (14 ounce) can pears
¼ cup cinnamon candies

8 drops red food coloring

Drain juice from pears into a medium saucepan. Add cinnamon candies and cook until candy melts. Add red food coloring and bring to a boil. Add pears and cook until soft but not mushy.

Coleslaw

1 carrot, chopped
⅓ medium green pepper, chopped
4½ cups shredded cabbage
1 cup water
½ cup mayonnaise

2 tablespoons sugar
2 tablespoons vinegar
Celery seed
Dill weed
Milk

Combine carrot, pepper, cabbage, and water in a blender. Drain. Mix mayonnaise, sugar, vinegar, and a dash of celery seed and dill weed together to make the dressing. Add enough milk to make the dressing creamy. Pour over vegetables and stir until well blended.

Cookie Cutter Sandwich

2 slices of bread
Deli meat, any kind
1 slice cheese, any kind
Lettuce (optional)

Pickle (optional)
Tomato (optional)
Onion (optional)

Put deli meat on bottom slice of bread and top with cheese. Add desired amount of lettuce, pickle, tomato, and onion. Top with second slice of bread and cut with cookie cutter to form desired shape.

Cranberry Fluff

1 cup cranberry juice
1 small box raspberry gelatin

1 cup whipped topping

Bring cranberry juice to a boil in a medium saucepan. Remove from heat and add gelatin; stir until dissolved. Pour into a 9x9-inch dish and chill until thickened. Fold in whipped topping and chill until firm.

Deviled Eggs
(from Wanda Royer)

12 eggs, hard boiled
½ teaspoon salt
1 teaspoon mustard

1 teaspoon vinegar
¼ cup mayonnaise
Paprika

Cut eggs in half lengthwise and carefully remove yolks. In a small mixing bowl, mash yolks and blend in salt, mustard, vinegar, and mayonnaise. Fill eggs with yolk mixture and sprinkle with paprika.

Easy Turkey and Broccoli Casserole

2 (10 ounce) packages frozen broccoli
spears
2 cups turkey, cooked and diced
1 cup cheddar cheese, shredded

1 (14½ ounce) can evaporated milk
1 (10½ ounce) can cream of chicken
soup
1 (3½ ounce) can french-fried
onions

Preheat oven to 350 degrees. Cook broccoli as directed on package. Layer turkey, broccoli, and cheese in a baking dish. Mix evaporated milk and soup together. Pour over ingredients in the baking dish. Bake for 25 minutes. Cover with onions and bake for 5 minutes. Serves 4 to 6.

Fancy Hot Dogs

8 hot dogs
1 (8 ounce) jar grape jelly

1 (8 ounce) jar cranberry sauce

Slice hot dogs into ½-inch pieces. Heat grape jelly and cranberry sauce over medium heat, stirring constantly until heated through. Add hot dog pieces and cook on low heat until hot dogs are hot. Serve with toothpicks.

Fried Green Beans

3 cups green beans
⅓ cup Italian dressing

2 tablespoons toasted almond
slivers (optional)

In a large skillet, cook green beans in half of the dressing until tender. Add remaining dressing to green beans and lightly mix. Pour in a serving dish and sprinkle with almonds.

Fruit Dip

1 cup cream cheese, softened   1 cup marshmallow fluff

In a mixing bowl, beat cream cheese and marshmallow fluff with an electric mixer until smooth. Spoon into a dish and serve with fresh fruit.

Fruit Salad

1 small box strawberry gelatin

1 (14½ ounce) canned fruit cocktail, drained

Prepare strawberry gelatin as directed on box. Add fruit cocktail to gelatin and stir. Pour into a 9x9-inch baking dish and refrigerate until firm.

Fruit Tray

2 apples
2 oranges
2 kiwis
2 bananas
2 peaches

2 cups strawberries
2 cups grapes
½ pineapple
Orange or lemon juice

Wash all fruit thoroughly, except bananas and pineapple. Slice fruit. Dip apple and banana slices in orange or lemon juice to keep them from turning brown. Arrange all fruit on a large serving dish. Serve with Fruit Dip (see recipe on page 43).

Green Spaghetti
(from Craig Preas)

1 pound ground beef
1 tablespoon garlic powder
1 (1 pound) box thin spaghetti noodles

8 drops green food coloring
1 (26½ ounce) jar spaghetti sauce

Brown ground beef and garlic in a skillet. Drain excess fat. Prepare spaghetti noodles as directed on box. Drain spaghetti. With spaghetti still in the pan, add food coloring and stir until spaghetti turns green. Heat spaghetti sauce and ground beef in a medium saucepan over medium heat until hot. Serve on top of green spaghetti noodles.

Green Stuff

(from Debbie Sindeldecker)

1 (20 ounce) can crushed pineapple, undrained
1 small box instant pistachio pudding
8 ounces whipped topping

1¼ cups mini marshmallows (or fruit-flavored mini marshmallows)
½ cup coconut, shredded (optional)

Pour pineapple with juice into large mixing bowl. Add pudding and mix well. Fold in whipped topping, marshmallows, and coconut. Place in serving bowl and refrigerate until firm.

Hawaiian Cheese Ball

(from Rebecca Germany)

1 (8 ounce) package cream cheese, softened
¼ cup cheese, shredded
½ teaspoon seasoned salt
¼ teaspoon onion powder

1 tablespoon green or red peppers, finely chopped
1 (8 ounce) can crushed pineapple, drained
¼ cup pecans, chopped

Mix all ingredients in a bowl, except pecans. Shape into a ball on plastic wrap. Roll in the pecans to cover completely. Place on a serving dish and store in refrigerator. Serve with crackers.

Hot Turkey Salad

2 cups turkey, cooked and diced
1 cup celery, diced
½ cup cheddar cheese, shredded
2 teaspoons onion powder

½ teaspoon salt
Pinch of pepper
¼ cup mayonnaise
8 hamburger buns, split and
    buttered

Preheat oven to 350 degrees. In a medium bowl, mix turkey, celery, cheese, onion powder, salt, pepper, and mayonnaise. Fill buns with turkey mixture. Wrap each sandwich in aluminum foil and place on an ungreased baking sheet. Bake for 20 minutes or until heated through. Makes 8 sandwiches.

Layered Salad

1 pound bacon
1 large head lettuce, rinsed, dried,
    and chopped
1 red onion, chopped
10 ounces cheddar cheese, shredded

1 cup cauliflower, chopped
1 cup broccoli, chopped
6 to 8 eggs, hard boiled
1¼ cups mayonnaise
2 tablespoons sugar

Cook bacon over medium heat in a large skillet. Crumble bacon and set aside. Place lettuce in a large, flat bowl and layer with onion, cheese, cauliflower, broccoli, eggs, and bacon. Mix mayonnaise and sugar; spoon over salad. Refrigerate until chilled.

Meat Tray

½ pound sliced ham
½ pound sliced turkey

½ pound sliced bologna
¼ pound sliced salami

Tightly roll each slice of meat. Arrange on serving tray.

Messy Buns

1 to 1½ pounds ground beef
½ cup ketchup
2 tablespoons mustard

2 tablespoons Worcestershire sauce
2 tablespoons brown sugar
8 hot dog buns

Brown ground beef in a skillet. Add remaining ingredients and simmer for 10 minutes. Fill hot dog buns with beef mixture. Serve while hot.

Pigs in a Blanket
(from Roy Royer)

1 can crescent roll dough   8 hot dogs

Preheat oven to 350 degrees. Flatten each triangle of crescent roll dough and wrap each triangle around a hot dog, sealing as much as possible. Place on an ungreased cookie sheet. Bake for 10 minutes or until dough is lightly brown.

Salsa Side Dip

1 (10 ounce) can diced tomatoes
with green chilies

1 (16 ounce) package cheddar cheese
Tortilla chips

Pour tomatoes with green chilies into a microwave-safe bowl. Cut cheese into cubes and add to tomatoes. Cook over low heat for 5 minutes. Stir until the cheese is mixed into tomatoes with green chilies. Serve with tortilla chips.

Scalloped Potatoes

1 (4.9 ounce) package scalloped potato
    mix
1⅔ cups boiling water

1 cup heavy cream
3 tablespoons butter
1 cup cheddar cheese, shredded

Heat oven to 450 degrees. In an ungreased 1½-quart casserole dish, stir potato mix and sauce. Add water, heavy cream, butter, and cheese. Bake uncovered for 20 minutes or until top is light golden brown and potatoes are tender. Remove from oven. Sauce will thicken as is stands.

Submarine Sandwich

8 sub rolls
Mayonnaise
Mustard
Deli meat, any kind

16 cheese slices, any kind
Lettuce leaves, 2 per sandwich
1 tomato, sliced
Pickles

Cut sub rolls in half lengthwise, but not all the way through. Spread mayonnaise, mustard, or other desired dressing on top half of bun. Add meat, cheese, lettuce, tomato, and pickles in layers on bottom bun. Add top bun.

For a heated sub sandwich, place in oven before adding lettuce, tomatoes, and pickles. Bake at 350 degrees for 10 minutes. Add lettuce, tomatoes, and pickles.

Sweet Carrots

1 (16 ounce) bag whole baby carrots
1 cup water
½ cup brown sugar
¼ teaspoon salt
1½ teaspoons cornstarch

1 tablespoon honey
1 tablespoon butter
1 (8 ounce) can crushed pineapple
  (keep juice)
1 tablespoon cinnamon

Preheat oven to 350 degrees. In a medium saucepan, cook carrots in water over medium heat for 10 minutes or until tender. In a small saucepan, combine brown sugar, salt, and cornstarch; cook over lower heat for 15 minutes, stirring constantly. Remove from heat and stir in honey and butter. Combine carrots and pineapple in a casserole dish and pour liquid mixture over carrots. Sprinkle with cinnamon. Bake for 40 minutes.

Turkey and Gravy Sandwich

1 (6 ounce) package stuffing mix
6 slices of bread

1 pound turkey breast, cooked
and sliced
1 (12 ounce) jar turkey gravy,
warmed

Prepare stuffing as directed on box. Place 1 slice of bread on each plate. Top with turkey and stuffing. Drizzle with gravy.

Vegetable Tray

3 stalks celery
1 cup radishes
1 green pepper
1 cucumber
2 cups baby carrots

2 cups broccoli
2 cups cauliflower
2 cups cherry tomatoes
1 cup ranch salad dressing

Thoroughly clean all vegetables. Cut celery stalks into 3-inch pieces. Cut radishes in half. Remove seeds from the green pepper and slice pepper lengthwise. Slice cucumber. Chop broccoli and cauliflower into bite-sized pieces. Arrange vegetables on large tray. Serve with ranch salad dressing.

Whipped Potatoes

²⁄₃ cup water
²⁄₃ cup heavy cream
¹⁄₄ teaspoon salt

2 tablespoons butter
²⁄₃ cup mashed potato flakes
3 tablespoons sour cream

Combine water, heavy cream, salt, and butter in a microwave-safe bowl. Microwave for approximately 2 minutes until mixture becomes foamy. Remove from microwave. Stir in potato flakes to moisten. Add sour cream and mix well. Serve while hot.

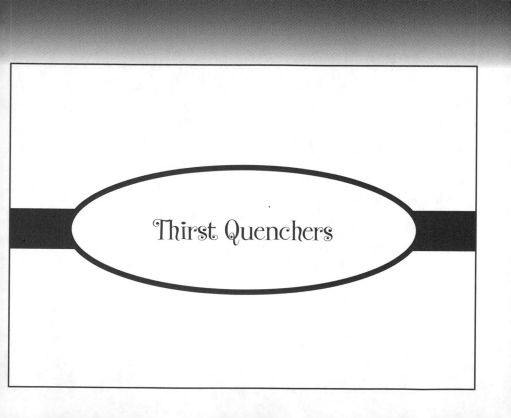

Legend of the First Christmas Tree

AUTHOR UNKNOWN

One wintry Christmas Eve, Martin Luther was traveling home through the woods. It was a clear, starry night, and the stars sparkled through the branches of the towering evergreen trees.

Martin Luther was amazed by the beauty of the sight and wished his wife and children could see it. So he cut down a small fir tree and brought it into his house. Then he put candles on the tree branches to shine like stars.

"Come see," he called to his wife and children. "This is how the stars shone down on Bethlehem long ago, when Jesus was born." And that was the very first Christmas tree.

Apple Pie Milk Shake

½ cup milk
½ cup apple pie filling or
   a slice of apple pie

1 cup vanilla ice cream
½ teaspoon ground cinnamon

Place all ingredients in a blender. Make sure lid is on tight and blend until smooth. Pour into glasses. Can use other flavors of ice cream and pie if desired.

Banana Blender Drink

1 banana
½ cup orange juice

½ cup milk
1 teaspoon honey

Put all ingredients into a blender and blend on high until smooth. Pour into glasses and enjoy!

Christmas Punch

1 (.13 ounce) package lemonade
   drink mix
1 (48 ounce) bottle cranberry-grape juice

1 (1 liter) bottle seltzer, chilled
1 orange, sliced and seeded

Pour lemonade drink mix into a pitcher and add cranberry-grape juice. Stir until drink mix is dissolved. Just before serving, add seltzer and orange slices.

Cinnamon Cider

1 quart apple cider   ¼ cup cinnamon candies

Pour apple cider into a large pot and add cinnamon candies. Heat and stir until candy melts and cider turns red. Pour into mugs and serve while hot.

Holiday Punch

½ gallon lime or raspberry sherbet

2 quarts ginger ale or other clear soda pop

Scoop sherbet into punch bowl. Slowly pour soda pop over the sherbet. Serve while cold.

Hot Chocolate

½ cup sugar
¼ cup unsweetened cocoa powder
⅓ cup hot water
4 cups milk
¾ teaspoon vanilla extract

Cinnamon stick or peppermint stick
Whipped topping (optional)
Caramel topping (optional)
Sprinkles (optional)
Maraschino cherries (optional)

Mix sugar and cocoa in a medium saucepan. Stir in water. Stirring constantly, cook over medium heat until mixture boils. After boiling for 2 minutes, add milk. Reduce heat and cook until hot, but do not boil. Remove from heat and add vanilla. Beat with whisk until foamy. Pour into mugs and add a cinnamon or peppermint stick. Top with whipped topping, caramel, sprinkles, and a cherry, if desired. Serves 4 to 6.

Iced Tea

4 cups water
3 family-sized tea bags or
   6 regular-sized tea bags

¾ cup sugar

Bring water to a boil on high heat in a medium saucepan. When water boils, add tea bags and remove from heat; cover for 10 minutes. Remove tea bags. Add sugar to a 1-gallon pitcher. Pour hot tea into pitcher. Fill pitcher with cold water and stir. Cover with lid and store in refrigerator.

Mint Cocoa

15 chocolate sandwich cookies,
   crushed
3 cups milk
⅓ cup chocolate syrup

¼ teaspoon peppermint extract
4 tablespoons whipped topping
4 pinches of cinnamon

Place sandwich cookies, milk, chocolate syrup, and peppermint extract in a blender and cover. Blend on high speed until well mixed. Pour into a medium saucepan and cook over medium heat until heated through. Pour into 4 mugs. Top each mug with 1 tablespoon whipped topping and a pinch of cinnamon.

Snowy Ice Drink

1 cold beverage (juice or soda)   Snow, clean

Fill glass with snow. Pour beverage over snow.

Strawberry Milk

1½ cups cold milk   2 teaspoons strawberry jam

Mix milk with strawberry jam in a blender or shaker and pour into a glass.

Minty Chocolate Milk

2 tablespoons chocolate syrup
⅛ teaspoon peppermint flavoring

1 cup milk
1 scoop chocolate ice cream

Stir together chocolate syrup, peppermint flavoring, and milk. Add ice cream.
Serve immediately.

Malted Milk Ball Chiller

⅓ cup malted milk balls, crushed
1 cup ice cream

1½ tablespoons chocolate syrup
½ cup milk

Place ingredients into blender and mix until creamy. Pour into a glass. Serve immediately.

Candy Cane Cocoa

4 cups milk
3 (1 ounce) squares semisweet
chocolate, chopped

4 peppermint candy canes, crushed
1 cup whipped cream
4 small peppermint candy canes

In a medium saucepan, heat milk until hot, but not boiling. Whisk in the chocolate and the crushed candy canes until smooth. Pour hot cocoa into 4 mugs. Serve each with a miniature candy cane stirring stick.

Festive Hot Cocoa

1 package instant cocoa
Whipped cream

Red and green candy sprinkles
1 cherry

Prepare instant cocoa as directed on package. Spoon whipped cream onto the mug of cocoa; top with candy sprinkles and a cherry.

Snowy Cinnamon Cocoa

4 cups milk
1 cup chocolate syrup
1 teaspoon ground cinnamon

Whipped topping
¼ cup semi-sweet chocolate chips

Place milk and chocolate syrup in a microwave-safe bowl and stir. Cook on high for 3 to 4 minutes or until hot. Stir in cinnamon. Pour into 4 large mugs and garnish with whipped topping and chocolate chips.

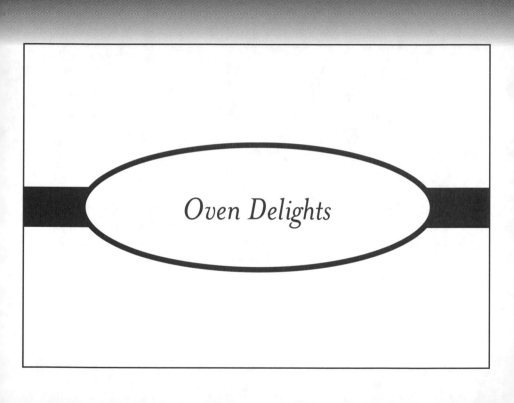

Oven Delights

The Star

AUTHOR UNKNOWN

A star led kings to find a Savior long ago in a far-off land. Their prince was found lying in a manger, signifying God's love for man. Each Christmas we give love to others; we have charity for everyone. Let us not just spread our love at Christmas, but continue when the season is gone. May the love we feel at Christmastime be known by others far and near.

Apple Cinnamon Bars

DOUGH:
- 2½ cups flour
- 1 teaspoon salt
- 1 cup shortening
- 1 egg yolk and water to make ⅔ cup

FILLING:
- 1 cup oatmeal
- 6 to 8 apples, cored, peeled, and sliced
- ¾ cup sugar
- 1 teaspoon cinnamon

TOPPING:
- 1 cup powdered sugar
- 4 to 5 teaspoons milk

Preheat oven to 350 degrees. Mix flour, salt, shortening, egg, and water together until dough forms. Roll out half the dough to fit a cookie sheet lined with waxed paper. Sprinkle dough with oatmeal, apples, sugar, and cinnamon. Cover with remaining rolled-out dough. Pinch edges together. Bake for 50 minutes. Mix powdered sugar and milk to make icing. Drizzle while still warm.

Baked Cinnamon Sugar Apples

4 apples
½ cup brown sugar

1 teaspoon cinnamon
4 tablespoons butter

Preheat oven to 350 degrees. Core apples and peel skin off a 1-inch strip around the stem end of each apple. Mix brown sugar and cinnamon in a small bowl. Stuff brown sugar and cinnamon mixture in apples and place apples in a shallow baking dish. Top each apple with 1 tablespoon butter and bake for 50 minutes or until apples are tender.

Brownie Wreath

1 large brownie mix
1 (16 ounce) can prepared frosting
Green food coloring

White sprinkles
Cinnamon candies

Mix brownies as directed on package. Pour batter in greased bundt cake pan.
Bake as directed on package. Cool completely. Remove brownie from pan and
place on a serving dish. Add a few drops of food coloring to the frosting and stir
until desired color appears. Spread frosting evenly over brownie and decorate
with sprinkles and cinnamon candies.

Cake Mix Cookies

1 lemon or strawberry cake mix
2 eggs

½ cup butter, softened
Powdered sugar

Preheat oven to 350 degrees. Mix dry cake mix with eggs and butter in a bowl. Form into 1-inch balls and place on cookie sheet. Bake for approximately 10 minutes. Do not overbake or cookies will be hard. Sprinkle cookies with powdered sugar while still warm.

Candy Cane Breadsticks

1 (11 ounce) can refrigerator breadsticks   ¾ cup parmesan cheese, grated
3 tablespoons butter, melted

Preheat oven to 350 degrees. Cut breadsticks in half; dip them in melted butter and sprinkle with cheese. Twist breadsticks together to form candy canes and place on an ungreased cookie sheet. Bake for 14 to 18 minutes or until light brown.

Chocolate Cookie Brownie Bars

1 large brownie mix

15 chocolate sandwich cookies, crushed

Prepare brownies as directed on package; stir crushed cookies into batter. Pour into a greased 9x13-inch pan. Bake as directed on package. Cool and cut into bars.

Easy Pecan Pie

2 eggs
½ cup sugar
½ cup corn syrup
2 tablespoons butter, melted

½ teaspoon vanilla
1½ cups pecan halves
9-inch unbaked piecrust

Preheat oven to 425 degrees. In a blender, blend eggs and sugar into a paste. Add corn syrup, butter, and vanilla to the paste and blend together. Add 1 cup of the halved pecans and blend until pecans are just chopped. Pour into the crust and bake for 15 minutes. Reduce heat to 350 degrees and bake for 25 additional minutes. When done, a butter knife will come out clean when stuck in the center. Top with additional pecans before serving.

Frosted Cake Snowballs

1 white cake mix
1 (16 ounce) can vanilla frosting

½ cup white chocolate chips

Prepare cake mix and bake as directed on package. While still warm, crumble cake in a bowl and stir in frosting. Melt chocolate chips in a saucepan on low heat. Roll cake into 1-inch balls and dip into melted chocolate chips. Place on waxed paper until cool.

Fudge Bars

1½ cups semisweet chocolate chips
1½ cups butterscotch chips

1 (7 ounce) can sweetened
    condensed milk
½ teaspoon vanilla

Melt chocolate chips, butterscotch chips, and milk in a saucepan on low heat, stirring until smooth. Remove from heat and add vanilla. Pour into an 8-inch pan and place in refrigerator until firm. Cut into 1-inch bars.

Gingerbread Kids

1 cup sugar
1 cup butter
1 teaspoon ground cinnamon
1 teaspoon ground cloves
1 teaspoon ground nutmeg
1 teaspoon ground ginger

½ cup molasses
1 teaspoon vinegar
2 eggs, beaten
5 cups flour, sifted
1 teaspoon baking soda

Preheat oven to 350 degrees. In a 1-quart saucepan, bring sugar, butter, cinnamon, cloves, nutmeg, ginger, and molasses to a boil, stirring constantly. Cool to lukewarm. Add vinegar and eggs. Mix well. Blend in flour and baking soda to form a smooth dough. Chill. Roll out on floured board and cut with a 4- to 6-inch gingerbread man cookie cutter. (Or any shape cookie cutter may be used.) Bake on an ungreased cookie sheet for 10 minutes.

Great-Grandma Royer's Sugar Cookies
(from Bessie Royer)

3 eggs, beaten
2 teaspoons vanilla
2 cups sugar
1 cup lard or shortening

1 cup milk
½ teaspoon baking soda
7 cups flour (approximately)
4 teaspoons baking powder

Preheat oven to 350 degrees. Mix eggs, vanilla, sugar, and lard until smooth. Blend milk and baking soda together before adding it to the mixture. Sift together flour and baking powder. Slowly add to the mixture until the dough is the right texture for handling. Roll dough out on a floured surface and cut into shapes with cookie cutters. Bake for 10 minutes.

Holiday Bread

1 cup water
1½ cups chopped dates
1 tablespoon butter
½ cup packed brown sugar
1 egg

½ cup buttermilk
1½ cups flour
¾ cup rolled oats
1 teaspoon baking soda
1 cup pecans, chopped

Preheat oven to 350 degrees. Bring water to a boil. Pour boiling water into a large bowl and add dates. After dates have moistened, add butter, brown sugar, egg, and buttermilk and stir until well blended. In another bowl, mix flour, oats, and baking soda together. Combine with other mixture and stir until well blended. Add pecans and stir again. Pour into a greased loaf pan and bake for 50 minutes.

Holiday Meringue Drops

4 egg whites
¼ teaspoon cream of tartar
¾ cup sugar

1 small box lime gelatin
1 small box strawberry or raspberry
gelatin

Combine egg whites and cream of tartar in a bowl. Beat on high for 5 minutes with an electric mixer. Add sugar, 1 tablespoon at a time. Drop batter by teaspoonfuls onto a greased cookie sheet. Sprinkle lime and strawberry gelatin over each drop and bake for 50 minutes. Turn oven off and remove when completely cool, approximately 1 hour.

Hot Rolls

1 (3 pound) bag frozen dinner rolls

Thaw rolls. Cut each roll into 3 parts, roll into balls, and drop into greased muffin tins. Cover with plastic wrap sprayed with nonstick vegetable spray. Let rise until the rolls double in size, about 2 to 3 hours. Bake at 350 degrees for 15 to 20 minutes or until brown. Place in a breadbasket and cover with a towel to keep warm. Store in an airtight container.

Mini Fruit Cookies

1 cup brown sugar
½ cup butter
1 egg
1 teaspoon vanilla
⅓ cup cherries, chopped
⅓ cup pineapple, chopped

⅓ cup flaked coconut
⅓ cup walnuts, chopped
2 cups flour
1 teaspoon baking powder
½ teaspoon baking soda
¼ teaspoon salt

Preheat oven to 375 degrees. Mix together brown sugar, butter, egg, and vanilla with an electric mixer. Add cherries, pineapple, coconut, and walnuts. Mix with a spoon. In a different bowl, mix flour, baking powder, baking soda, and salt. Add to the fruit mixture. Stir well. Drop cookies onto a greased cookie sheet about 1 inch apart. Bake for 10 to 12 minutes. Remove the cookies immediately from the cookie sheet to cool.

Oatmeal Bars

¾ cup brown sugar
½ cup light corn syrup
2 teaspoons vanilla

½ cup melted butter
⅔ cup peanut butter

Combine above ingredients in a bowl and mix with an electric mixer.

3 cups oatmeal
½ cup coconut

½ cup sunflower seeds
¾ cup miniature semisweet
   chocolate chips

Add to above mixture and stir with a spoon. Preheat oven to 350 degrees. Pour into a lightly greased 9x13-inch pan. Bake for 15 to 20 minutes. Cut into squares while warm.

Peanut Butter Candy Cookies

½ cup shortening
¾ cup peanut butter
⅓ cup sugar
⅓ cup brown sugar
1 egg
2 tablespoons milk

1 teaspoon vanilla
1½ cups flour
1 teaspoon baking soda
½ teaspoon salt
1 (8 ounce) bag chocolate kisses,
    unwrapped

Preheat oven to 375 degrees. Beat shortening and peanut butter in a large bowl until well blended. Add sugar and brown sugar and beat until fluffy. Add egg, milk, and vanilla; beat well. Stir together flour, baking soda, and salt. Gradually beat into peanut butter mixture. Drop by tablespoonfuls onto an ungreased cookie sheet. Bake for 8 to 10 minutes or until brown. Immediately press chocolate candy into the center of each cookie and remove cookies from the cookie sheet. Cool completely on a wire rack.

Peanut Butter Cup Brownies
(from Debbie Sindeldecker)

1 large brownie mix

Miniature peanut butter cups, unwrapped

Preheat oven to 350 degrees. Prepare brownie mixture as directed on package. Fill greased mini muffin cups ⅔ full. Press peanut butter cup into the center of each muffin cup. Do not overflow. Bake for 10 to 15 minutes. Do not overbake.

Peanut Butter Drops

1 (12 ounce) package peanut butter chips
1 cup peanut butter

4 cups cornflakes cereal
½ cup cocktail peanuts

Melt peanut butter chips and peanut butter over low heat, stirring constantly. Remove from heat and stir in cereal and peanuts until well coated. Drop by spoonfuls onto waxed paper. Cool until set.

Peanut Butter and Jelly Cookies

3 cups flour
1 cup sugar
1 teaspoon baking soda
½ teaspoon salt
1½ cups peanut butter

½ cup butter, melted
½ cup honey
2 tablespoons milk
½ cup jelly, any flavor

Preheat oven to 375 degrees. Combine flour, sugar, baking soda, and salt in a large bowl. Add peanut butter and butter with an electric mixer until crumbly. Stir in honey and milk. Form into 1-inch balls and place on an ungreased cookie sheet. Press thumb in the middle of each and fill with 1 tablespoon jelly. Bake for 8 to 10 minutes.

Pecan Sugar Balls

½ cup butter
2 tablespoons honey
½ teaspoon vanilla

1 cup flour
2 cups pecan pieces
Red or green sugar crystals

Preheat oven to 350 degrees. Mix butter and honey in a bowl with an electric mixer. Add vanilla, flour, and pecans. Stir well. Form into 1-inch balls and place on an ungreased cookie sheet. Bake for 12 to 14 minutes. Cool slightly and roll in sugar crystals.

Snickerdoodles

1 cup shortening
1½ cups sugar
2 eggs
2¾ cups flour

2 teaspoons cream of tartar
1 teaspoon baking soda
½ teaspoon salt
4 tablespoons cinnamon sugar

Preheat oven to 375 degrees. Mix shortening and sugar in a bowl with an electric mixer. Add eggs and mix well. Mix flour, cream of tartar, baking soda, and salt in a second bowl. Add dry ingredients to egg mixture and mix well; let stand in the refrigerator until cool. Combine cinnamon and sugar in a small bowl. Roll dough into 1-inch balls, then roll balls in cinnamon sugar. Place on a greased cookie sheet and bake for 8 to 10 minutes. Do not overbake.

Snowball Cupcakes

1 white cake mix
1 (16 ounce) can white frosting

2 cups flaked coconut

Heat oven to 350 degrees. Line muffin tins with paper liners. Mix cake as directed on package. Fill muffin tins ⅔ full and bake as directed on package. When cool, remove from the tin and coat with frosting, then dip each cupcake in coconut.

Snow-Covered Brownies

4 eggs
2 cups sugar
1½ cups flour
½ cup unsweetened cocoa powder

1 teaspoon vanilla
1 cup butter, melted
½ cup powdered sugar

Preheat oven to 350 degrees. Combine all ingredients except powdered sugar; mix well. Pour into a greased and floured 9x13-inch pan. Bake for 25 minutes. Do not overbake. Sprinkle powdered sugar over cooled brownies. Cut into squares.

Sugar Cookie Icing

1 cup powdered sugar
⅛ teaspoon salt
½ teaspoon vanilla

1 tablespoon water
Few drops food coloring (optional)
Sprinkles (optional)

Mix powdered sugar, salt, vanilla, and water together. If color is wanted, stir food coloring into the mixture. Spread on cookie and then immediately put sprinkles on. If icing is too hard, add a few drops of water and stir. Allow the icing to harden on cookies before storing in an airtight container.

Twisted Cookies

1 cup butter
1 cup powdered sugar
1 egg
2½ cups flour

½ teaspoon salt
½ teaspoon red food coloring
Sugar

Preheat oven to 350 degrees. Blend butter, sugar, and egg in a bowl. Add flour and salt. Divide the dough in half. Color one half red with food coloring and leave the other half white. Chill for about an hour. Roll into 4-inch ropes and twist together to make candy canes. Bake for 9 to 11 minutes. Sprinkle with sugar to make them sparkle.

Winter S'mores

1 large brownie mix
1 cup mini marshmallows

8 graham crackers, plain or
cinnamon

Prepare and bake brownies as directed on the package. Five minutes before the baking time expires, spread marshmallows evenly over the brownies. Arrange graham crackers to fit evenly over the marshmallows. Bake for an additional 5 minutes.

Nutty Caramel Corn

12 cups popped popcorn
3 cups almonds
1 cup brown sugar, packed
½ cup margarine

¼ cup light corn syrup
½ teaspoon salt
½ teaspoon baking soda

Preheat oven to 200 degrees. Divide popcorn and almonds between 2 ungreased 9x13-inch baking dishes. Heat brown sugar, margarine, corn syrup, and salt until mixture simmers; stir constantly. Remove from heat and add baking soda. Pour mixture over the popped corn; stir until coated well. Bake for 1 hour, stirring every 15 minutes.

No-Bake Treats

The Christmas Story:
The Birth of Jesus

(PARAPHRASED FROM THE BIBLE, MATTHEW 2:1–11 AND LUKE 1:26–38 AND 2:1–20)

Once, long ago,
an angel came to Mary and said,
"You will have a baby boy,
and you will name Him Jesus.
He will be very great
and will be called the Son of God."

And so, when the time came,
Mary and Joseph rode on a donkey
to the little town of Bethlehem.
There was no room for them at the inn,
so Jesus was born in a barn.

Mary wrapped Him in a blanket
and laid Him in a manger.

That night,
shepherds were watching their sheep
in the fields.
Suddenly an angel came to them and said,
"I bring you news of great joy!
A Savior—Christ the Lord—
has been born!"

The angel was joined by many other angels, singing,
"Glory to God in the highest!
Peace on earth, goodwill to men!"
The shepherds said to each other,
"Come! Let's go see this wonderful thing!"
They ran to Bethlehem,
and found the baby Jesus lying in a manger.

Also that night,
three wise men from the East saw a bright star.
They were filled with joy!
They followed the star.
The star led them to the baby Jesus.
The wise men fell down and worshiped Him,
and gave him gifts.

And now, every Christmas we, too, worship Jesus, our Savior, and celebrate His birth!

Happy Birthday, Jesus!

Almond Chocolate Brittle

2 cups white chocolate chips
1 tablespoon vegetable oil

½ cup chopped almonds

Line an 8x8-inch square baking dish with foil. In a saucepan, on low heat, melt together white chocolate chips and vegetable oil. Stir until melted. Add almonds. Pour into a pan and refrigerate until firm. Break into pieces. Store in an airtight container.

Apples on a Stick

6 medium apples
6 Popsicle sticks
1 (14 ounce) package caramels,
   unwrapped

3 tablespoons milk
¼ cup creamy peanut butter
6 tablespoons unsalted peanuts,
   chopped

Wash apples and remove stems. Poke Popsicle sticks into the stem ends. Heat caramels, milk, and peanut butter in a microwave-safe dish until melted, approximately 2 minutes. Dip each apple in the caramel mixture until completely coated. Roll in chopped peanuts. Refrigerate for about 1 hour until coating is firm.

Buckeyes

4 cups peanut butter
3½ cups powdered sugar
½ cup butter, softened

2¼ cups semisweet chocolate chips
1 tablespoon vegetable oil

Mix peanut butter, powdered sugar, and butter in a bowl. Form into 1-inch balls. Melt chocolate chips with oil over low heat. Using a toothpick, dip the top of the peanut butter balls in the melted chocolate, leaving a little bit of peanut butter showing on the top. Place on waxed paper until firm.

Candy Cane Heart

2 candy canes, wrapped
Hot glue

Red ribbon or red lace licorice

Lay two candy canes flat on a table facing each other to form a heart. Using a hot glue gun, glue the top and bottom of the candy canes together. Use the ribbon to tie around the top of the heart to make hanger. To make it an edible ornament, take the plastic off the candy canes and use sugar cookie icing recipe on page 105 as glue; use licorice for the ribbon.

Caramel-Covered Pretzel Twists

¼ cup semisweet chocolate chips
¼ cup peanut butter chips
2 tablespoons chopped walnuts

1 bag pretzel twists
1 (8 ounce) jar caramel topping

Combine chocolate chips, peanut butter chips, and walnuts in a food processor, crushing into medium chunks. Dip pretzels in caramel and then in the chip and nut mixture. Lay on waxed paper until caramel has thickened.

Cereal Party Mix

6 tablespoons butter
1½ teaspoons seasoned salt
2 tablespoons Worcestershire sauce
5 cups rice cereal

4 cups corn cereal
1 cup cocktail peanuts
1 cup mini pretzels

Melt butter on high for 1 minute in a large microwave-safe bowl. Stir in seasoned salt and Worcestershire sauce. Gradually add cereals, peanuts, and pretzels. Stir until all pieces are evenly coated. Microwave on high for 6 minutes, stirring every 2 minutes. Store in an airtight container.

Cherry Drops

2 (16 ounce) jars stemmed cherries
2 pounds powdered sugar
1 (14 ounce) can sweetened condensed
   milk

1 (24 ounce) package semisweet
   chocolate chips
¼ paraffin wax bar

Drain cherries and do not remove the stems. Mix powdered sugar and milk until mixture gets stiff. Cover cherries in the sugar mixture. Place cherries on waxed paper and put in the refrigerator overnight. The next day, melt the chocolate chips and wax on very low heat; remove from heat when completely melted. Dip cherries in melted chocolate chips and place back on waxed paper; refrigerate until chocolate has hardened.

Chocolate Caramel Cookies

1 (18 ounce) package refrigerated
  chocolate chip cookie dough
1 cup pecans, chopped

20 caramels, unwrapped
2 tablespoons milk

Preheat oven to 375 degrees. Place cookie dough in a bowl and stir in chopped pecans. Shape into 1-inch balls and place on a cookie sheet; bake for 8 to 10 minutes. While cookies are baking, melt caramels with milk on low heat in a small saucepan. Place cookies on waxed paper to cool; drizzle caramel and milk mixture over baked cookies.

Chocolate-Covered Crackers

1½ cups semisweet chocolate chips
1 tablespoon shortening

3 dozen peanut butter sandwich
    crackers

Combine chocolate chips and shortening in a 1-quart saucepan and cook over low heat until melted. Remove from heat; using a fork, dip crackers into mixture until coated. Place on a cookie sheet covered in waxed paper and chill until chocolate is hard. If chocolate gets hard while dipping, place chocolate back on burner on low heat to remelt.

Chocolate Pretzel Rings

4 dozen pretzel circles
1 (8 ounce) package milk chocolate
    kisses, unwrapped

50 candy coated chocolate pieces

Preheat oven to 275 degrees. Cover a cookie sheet with waxed paper. Spread pretzels on the cookie sheet. Place a kiss in the center of each pretzel. Bake for 2 to 3 minutes until chocolate is softened. Immediately place a coated candy on each chocolate and press down lightly so that chocolate spreads to touch pretzel. Refrigerate until chocolate is firm. Store at room temperature.

Christmas Tree Cones

Green food coloring
1 can white frosting
12 pointed sugar ice cream cones
Holiday sprinkles

Cinnamon candies and other
   toppings
Gumdrops
Red and white sparkling sugars

Stir food coloring into frosting until desired color appears. Spread frosting on each cone. Press sprinkles and other desired decorations into the frosting. Place a gumdrop on the top to resemble the star. Place on a wire cooling rack with waxed paper under it. Sprinkle with colored sugars.

Cookie Cutter Gelatin

2½ cups juice, any flavor   2 large boxes gelatin, any flavor

Bring the juice to a boil and add gelatin, stirring until dissolved. Pour into a 9x13-inch pan and refrigerate until firm. When ready to cut into shapes, place the bottom of the pan in warm water for about 15 seconds. Cut out the shapes, making sure to cut all the way through. Remove shapes and place on serving dish.

Cookie Truffles
(from Lisa Rovenstine)

1 (1 pound) package chocolate sandwich cookies, crushed

1 (8 ounce) package cream cheese, softened

1 pound milk chocolate candy coating, melted

¼ cup white candy coating or white chocolate chips, melted

In a large mixing bowl, combine crushed cookies and cream cheese to form a stiff dough. Shape into balls. Using a toothpick, dip balls into melted milk chocolate candy coating. Place on a wire rack over waxed paper in a cool area until set. To decorate the top with white chocolate, pour melted white candy coating in a plastic bag, cut a tiny hole in one corner, and drizzle over the top of each cookie ball.

Crispy Stockings

¼ cup butter
1 (10.5 ounce) package mini
marshmallows

1 (13 ounce) package chocolate
crispy or fruit crispy cereal

Melt butter and marshmallows in a large saucepan over low heat, stirring constantly until butter and marshmallows are melted. Remove from heat. Stir in cereal until evenly coated. Form about ⅓ cup cereal mixture into a stocking shape. Place on waxed paper to harden. May also shape into trees and wreaths.

Crunchy Noodle Drops

3 cups butterscotch chips
(or chocolate chips)

1¼ cups chow mein noodles
1 cup peanuts

Melt butterscotch chips on low heat, stirring constantly until melted. Remove from heat. Stir in noodles and peanuts until well coated. Drop by spoonfuls on waxed paper and let cool.

Cutout Crackers

1 package round crispy crackers   Deli cheese
Deli meat

Place a cracker on a plate. Use a holiday cookie cutter to cut shapes in deli meat
and cheese. Stack meat and cheese on cracker.

Dipped Candy Canes

Green food coloring
2 cups white chocolate chips, melted
12 candy canes

Sprinkles
Colored sugar crystals

Add green food coloring to melted chocolate until desired color appears. Dip the end of each candy cane, about 2 to 3 inches, into the green coating. Sprinkle with desired toppings and place on waxed paper until chocolate is firm.

Dirty Snowballs

1¼ cups flaked coconut
¾ cup butter, melted
1 pound powdered sugar

2 cups pecans, finely chopped
1 (6 ounce) package semisweet
chocolate chips

Mix coconut, butter, powdered sugar, and pecans together in a bowl. Roll dough into 1-inch balls and place in the refrigerator until chilled. Melt chocolate chips and, using a toothpick, dip each ball into melted chocolate. Place on waxed paper and chill until chocolate has hardened.

Edible Apple Ornament

4 to 6 medium apples
Popsicle sticks
Peanut butter

Chocolate sprinkles
Peanuts, finely chopped

Wash apples. Remove stems and poke Popsicle sticks into bottoms of apples.
Spread peanut butter evenly over apples. Decorate with sprinkles and peanuts.
Wrap individually in plastic wrap until ready to serve.

Fried Snowflakes

8 flour tortillas
Butter

Powdered sugar or cinnamon sugar

Fold tortilla into quarters. Cut pieces out of tortilla (as you would with a paper snowflake). Spread butter evenly on each side of tortilla. Fry tortilla in a frying pan until lightly browned. Sprinkle with powdered sugar or cinnamon sugar.

Frozen Pudding Pops

1 package instant vanilla pudding   Popsicle sticks
2 cups cold milk

Whisk together pudding and cold milk. Pour into paper cups. Place in freezer.
When partially frozen, put a Popsicle stick into the middle. Freeze until firm.
Remove from paper cups and serve. Can use any flavor instant pudding.

Frozen Raspberry Cups

1 small box raspberry gelatin
6 paper cups

1 pint mint chocolate chip ice cream

Prepare gelatin as directed on the box. Pour into paper cups and place in the freezer until frozen. When cups are completely frozen, place a scoop of ice cream on the top.

Frozen Strawberry Pie

CRUST:

1¼ cups pretzels, crushed

¼ cup sugar

2 tablespoons butter, softened

FILLING:

⅓ cup lime juice

1½ cups strawberries, crushed

1 (7 ounce) can sweetened
    condensed milk

8 ounces whipped topping

In a small bowl, mix all ingredients for crust and press into a 9-inch pie plate.
Refrigerate. In another bowl, mix lime juice, strawberries, and milk until well
blended. Fold in whipped topping. Pour into crust. Freeze until firm.

Gelatin Blocks

2 tablespoons gelatin
1¼ cups water
2 cups sugar

Food coloring
Powdered sugar

Stir gelatin into ½ cup cold water. Add sugar to ¾ cup water and boil for 5 minutes, stirring frequently. Add gelatin water to sugar water and boil for 15 minutes. Soak 3 shallow baking dishes in cold water. Divide gelatin mixture into 3 portions and color with desired food coloring. Pour into shallow pans and leave in the refrigerator for several hours until firm. Let set at room temperature for 15 minutes. Remove from the pan and cut into squares; coat with powdered sugar. Serve.

Holiday Popcorn

8 cups popped popcorn
¼ cup butter
¼ cup light corn syrup

½ cup sugar
1 small box strawberry or lime
gelatin

Preheat oven to 300 degrees. Line a cookie sheet with waxed paper. Pour popcorn into a large bowl and set aside. In a saucepan, melt butter and corn syrup over low heat, stirring constantly. Add sugar and gelatin; stir until gelatin is dissolved. Bring mixture to a boil and simmer for 5 minutes. Pour over the popcorn mixture and stir until well coated. Pour onto a cookie sheet and bake for 10 minutes. Remove from the oven and cool. Remove from the pan and break into small pieces. Store in an airtight container.

Ice Cream Snowballs

Favorite flavor ice cream   Flaked coconut

With clean hands, shape ice cream into any size snowballs. Roll in a bowl of
flaked coconut. Freeze until ready to eat.

Iced Graham Crackers

1 package graham crackers,
   plain or cinnamon

1 can frosting, any flavor
Sprinkles (optional)

Spread frosting over graham crackers. Top with sprinkles. Serve with hot cocoa.

Nibble Mix

3 cups mini wheat cereal
2 cups popped popcorn
1 cup mini pretzels

¼ cup butter, melted
1 tablespoon Worcestershire sauce
½ teaspoon seasoned salt

Stir cereal, popcorn, and pretzels in a microwave-safe bowl. Mix butter, Worcestershire sauce, and salt in another small bowl. Pour over the cereal mixture and stir until coated. Cook in the microwave for 2 to 3 minutes, stirring after 2 minutes. Stir until well coated. Serve.

No-Bake Cookies

2 cups sugar
1/4 cup unsweetened cocoa powder
1/4 cup butter
1/2 cup milk

1/2 cup peanut butter
1 teaspoon vanilla
2 1/2 cups flaked coconut

In a large saucepan, combine sugar, cocoa, butter, and milk. Bring to a boil for 1 minute. Remove from heat. Stir in peanut butter, vanilla, and coconut. Drop by teaspoonfuls onto waxed paper. Cool.

No-Cook Peanut Butter Balls

12 tablespoons peanut butter
6 tablespoons brown sugar
6 tablespoons powdered sugar

18 tablespoons maple syrup
6 tablespoons sugar
2 tablespoons vanilla

In a large bowl, mix all ingredients together and stir until stiff, adding more powdered sugar if not stiff. Roll into 1-inch balls and dip in powdered sugar. Refrigerate until firm. Makes 80 balls.

Peanut Butter Pie

24 peanut butter sandwich cookies
½ cup butter, melted
1 (8 ounce) package cream cheese,
    softened

1 cup peanut butter
½ cup sugar
1 tablespoon vanilla
8 ounces whipped topping

Crush the sandwich cookies into little pieces. Add butter and mix well. Press into a 9-inch pie plate. Mix cream cheese, peanut butter, sugar, and vanilla in a medium bowl with an electric mixer. Stir in whipped topping and pour into the piecrust. Freeze for 4 hours or until firm. Store in refrigerator.

Peanut Butter Play-Dough

2 cups peanut butter
6 tablespoons honey

Nonfat dry milk
Red or green food coloring

Mix peanut butter and honey together. Add enough nonfat dry milk to make dough workable. Add a few drops of food coloring. Roll out and cut into desired shapes. Store in an airtight container. If you keep it clean, you can eat it, too!

Peppermint Candy

6 candy canes   1½ cups white chocolate chips

Line a cookie sheet with waxed paper. Crush candy canes into small pieces. Melt chocolate chips in a medium saucepan over low heat, stirring constantly. Remove pan from heat. Add candy cane pieces to white chocolate and stir together. Pour onto cookie sheet and let stand until firm, about an hour. Break into pieces. Store in an airtight container.

Reindeer Food

4 cups toasted oats cereal
4 cups corn and rice cereal
2 cups pretzel sticks
1 cup nuts

1½ pounds white chocolate
1 teaspoon shortening
1 (12 ounce) package chocolate-
coated candies

Mix cereals, pretzels, and nuts in a bowl. Melt chocolate and shortening together on low heat in a large saucepan. Remove from heat. Add cereal mixture to melted chocolate. Stir until well coated. Add chocolate-coated candies. Stir until completely coated. Spread in thin layers on two cookie sheets. Cool in freezer until chocolate is hardened. Break into small pieces. Store in an airtight container.

Reindeer Heads

1 package peanut-shaped peanut
   butter sandwich cookies
64 pretzel sticks

Peanut butter
64 semisweet chocolate chips
32 cinnamon candies

Place sandwich cookies on waxed paper. Dip ends of two pretzel sticks in peanut butter. Attach to the top of sandwich cookie to look like antlers. To make antlers fuller, break a few pretzel sticks and dip them in peanut butter and add to first stick. Dip 2 chocolate chips in the peanut butter and stick on the cookie for eyes. Dip a cinnamon candy in the peanut butter and place on cookie for the nose.

Snow-Covered Pretzels

1 (1½ pound) package white chocolate   1 bag mini pretzels
   chips

Melt chocolate chips on low heat, stirring constantly. Drop pretzels into melted
chocolate a few at a time and turn until covered completely. Remove pretzels
with tongs and place on waxed paper until firm.

Snow Mix

1 cup semisweet chocolate chips
½ cup peanut butter
¼ cup butter

¼ teaspoon vanilla
9 cups corn and rice cereal
1½ cups powdered sugar

Combine chocolate chips, peanut butter, and butter in a large microwave-safe bowl. Microwave on high for 1 to 1½ minutes until smooth, stirring after 1 minute. Stir in vanilla. Pour in cereal, stirring until all pieces are evenly coated. Place cereal mixture and powdered sugar in a large plastic bag. Close bag and shake until well coated. Add more powdered sugar if cereal is not completely coated. Store in an airtight container.

Sweet and Salty Mix
(from Debbie Sindeldecker)

4 cups sweet and salty snack mix
    with cereal and pretzels
2 cups cheese crackers (squares
    or fish)

3 cups cone-shaped corn chips
1 cup peanuts or mixed nuts
1 cup chocolate-coated candies

In a large bowl, lightly toss all ingredients. Serve in small snack bowls. Store in an airtight container.

Whipped Pumpkin Dip

1 (8 ounce) package cream cheese,
  softened
1 (15 ounce) can pure pumpkin
1 (3 ounce) package instant vanilla
  pudding
2 teaspoons pumpkin pie spice
1 teaspoon ground cinnamon
8 ounces whipped topping
Cinnamon teddy bear–shaped
  cookies

Using an electric mixer, beat cream cheese until smooth. Add pumpkin, pudding,
pumpkin pie spice, and cinnamon. Mix well. Stir in whipped topping and spoon
into a bowl. Serve with cookies.

Winter Fudge

1 (12 ounce) package white chocolate
   chips
1 (18 ounce) jar peanut butter

1 (14 ounce) can sweetened
   condensed milk

Combine white chocolate chips and peanut butter in a microwave-safe bowl.
Heat on high for 3 minutes or until melted. Stir in sweetened condensed milk
until well blended. Press into a 9-inch baking pan and cool. Slice into squares
and serve with a glass of milk.

Yummy Pretzel Sticks

1 (15 ounce) package pretzel sticks
⅔ cup peanut oil

1 (1 ounce) package garlic and herb
   salad dressing mix
2 dashes salt

In a large mixing bowl, combine pretzels, peanut oil, salad dressing mix, and salt.
Mix thoroughly to coat all pretzels.

Cookies and Cream Pie

1 (3.9 ounce) package instant chocolate pudding mix
1 (8 ounce) container whipped topping, thawed
1½ cup chocolate sandwich cookies, crushed
1 (9 inch) prepared chocolate crumb piecrust

Prepare the pudding as directed on the package for pie filling; allow to set. When the pudding is ready, fold in the whipped topping. Add the crushed cookies; stir. Pour mixture into the prepared piecrust. Freeze pie until firm. Thaw in the refrigerator before serving.

Gingerbread House

Empty milk carton (the small kind
    you get at school)
5 graham crackers
White icing

Different kinds of candy (licorice,
    gumdrops, chocolate pieces,
    caramels, etc.)
Toothpicks

Use a spoon to smooth the icing on one side of a graham cracker. Place the
graham cracker, icing-side down, onto one side of the milk carton. Repeat this
step for the other three sides. For the roof of your house, break a graham cracker
in half before covering with icing (and use just the halves for the diagonal sides
of the roof). To decorate your house, use a toothpick to place icing on the candy
pieces. Then stick them onto your gingerbread house.

Chocolate Delight

1 package (4 serving size) instant
   chocolate pudding
2 cups milk
2 cups whipped topping, thawed

Chocolate garnish (chocolate chips,
   grated chocolate, chocolate
   cookie crumbs) or strawberries

Prepare pudding with milk as directed on package. Fold 1½ cups whipped
topping into pudding; spoon into 4 dessert dishes. Top with remaining ½ cup
whipped topping and chocolate garnish or strawberries.

Chocolate Chip Cheeseball

1 (8 ounce) package cream cheese,
  softened
½ cup butter, softened
¾ cup powdered sugar
2 tablespoons brown sugar

¼ teaspoon vanilla extract
¾ cup miniature semisweet
  chocolate chips
¾ cup pecans, finely chopped

In a medium bowl, combine cream cheese and butter. Beat with an electric hand mixer, on low speed, until smooth. Stir in powdered sugar, brown sugar, and vanilla. Add chocolate chips; stir. Cover and refrigerate for 2 hours. Form the chilled mixture into the shape of a ball. Wrap in plastic wrap and refrigerate for another hour. Roll the ball in the chopped pecans. Keep refrigerated until ready to serve.

No-Bake Christmas Graham Fudge

1 (12 ounce) package semisweet
   chocolate chips
¼ cup butter or margarine
2½ cups graham cracker crumbs

1½ cups almonds or pecans, chopped
1 (14 ounce) can sweetened
   condensed milk
1 teaspoon vanilla extract

Melt chocolate chips and butter together until smooth. In a large bowl, combine graham cracker crumbs and nuts. Stir in sweetened condensed milk and vanilla extract until crumbs are moistened, then stir in chocolate mixture until mixed well. Pat evenly into a greased 9x13-inch pan. Let stand at room temperature for 2 hours before cutting into squares.

Traditional No-Bake Cookies

½ cup (1 stick) butter or margarine
½ cup milk
2 cups sugar
½ cup unsweetened cocoa powder

1 cup peanut butter
1 teaspoon vanilla
3 cups oats

Combine butter, milk, sugar, and cocoa powder in a large saucepan. Bring to a rolling boil. Boil for 3 minutes (do not over boil); add peanut butter, vanilla, and oats; stir well. Drop by heaping teaspoonfuls onto a sheet of waxed paper. Let cool until firm. Store in an airtight container in a cool, dry place.

Peace on earth
will come to stay when
we live Christmas every day.

HELEN STEINER RICE